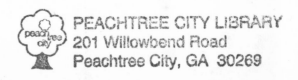

WE
THE PEOPLE
SUSAN B. ANTHONY

Library of Congress Cataloging-in-Publication Data

Klingel, Cindy.
  Susan B. Anthony.

  (We the people)
  Summary: A biography of Susan B. Anthony, who spent
her life tirelessly working so that women would have
rights equal to men's in the United States.
  1. Anthony, Susan B. (Susan Brownell), 1820-1906—
Juvenile literature.   2. Feminists—United States—
Biography—Juvenile literature.   3. Suffragettes—United
States—Biography—Juvenile literature.   [1. Anthony,
Susan B. (Susan Brownell), 1820-1906.   2. Feminists]
I. Title.   II. Series.
HQ1413.A55K56 1987   324.6'23'0924 [B] [92]   87-24650
ISBN 0-88682-164-9

WE
THE PEOPLE
SUSAN B. ANTHONY

CRUSADER FOR WOMEN'S RIGHTS
(1820-1906)

CINDY KLINGEL

Illustrated By John Keely & Dick Brude

CREATIVE EDUCATION

SUSAN B. ANTHONY

Susan B. Anthony was one of eight children. Her father, Daniel Anthony, had a small cotton mill. Her mother worked at the mill. All the looms at the mill were run by young women. These were the first women factory hands in Adams, Massachusetts.

Many of the factory girls lived in the Anthony house. Susan's mother had to cook for them, as well as take care of her children. The mill girls worked from six in the morning until six at night. But Mrs. Anthony worked harder— and longer.

Susan had to help her mother with the housework, and Susan was sad to see how hard a grown woman's life was. Poor Mrs. Anthony was a silent woman who seemed crushed by her labors. Susan helped, of course. There was little time for play. Susan and her sisters had to cook, clean, sew, wash, iron, and care for the garden and chickens.

When she was twelve years old

and her father needed temporary help at the mill, Susan begged to work for him. He agreed. Susan worked for two weeks. She saved the money she made and bought a set of blue cups and saucers for her mother. Susan was very proud when she presented her gift to her mother.

Susan's family followed the Quaker religion. Unlike society in general, the Quaker people believed that girls should have the same opportunities for schooling that boys had. Susan was intelligent and enjoyed school.

In 1838, when Susan was eighteen years old, her father lost his mill. Susan had to go to work to help the family. In those days, there were only a few ways a woman could earn a living; she could sew, work in a factory, be a servant, or she could teach.

Well-educated Susan became a teacher. She earned two dollars a week. It was much less than a man would be paid for the same work. This frustrated Susan, but she had no choice.

Susan was a bright, friendly young woman who enjoyed being with others. Many men admired Susan and proposed marriage. But she turned them down. A wife had no rights before the law. Her husband all but owned her. She could not have property of her own, could not even keep any money she earned herself. Men could mistreat their wives if they wanted to.

Quote

event

"I won't be any man's slave," declared Susan B. Anthony. All this time, Susan was becoming increasingly aware of the lack of rights women had. This affected her relationships with men.

Black slavery was a burning issue in the United States at this time. Susan met Frederick Douglass, who had been a slave. He told her how he and other abolitionists were working to wipe out slavery in the United States. Many women attended the meetings and speeches Mr. Douglass gave. Susan was surprised and impressed by these women who spoke out against slavery and voiced their opinions.

Susan took up the anti-slavery cause. She began to attend meet-

event

ings. She also was interested in the growing temperance movement. She knew many women who had suffered because of drunken men.

In 1849, Susan made her first public speech at a temperance meeting. People were amazed at her boldness. The men who listened were surprised that a "mere woman" could speak with such force.

The times were changing very quickly. In other parts of the East, women were beginning to demand legal rights. Susan heard of two speakers, Elizabeth Cady Stanton and Lucy Stone, who were insisting that colleges be opened to women. She met them in 1851. They shared the same beliefs, goals, and dreams. They agreed that in order to make

any changes to improve life for women, women needed to obtain the right to vote. From their meeting was born the organized movement for women's rights in the United States. Finally, Susan knew what she wanted to do with her life. She would work for equal rights for all people, regardless of sex or color, her main goal being to obtain the right for women to vote.

Susan decided to wear a new-style, comfortable dress, named after Amelia Bloomer. The dress was very loose and gathered at the ankles. It was very different from the tight dress usually worn. Very few women were brave enough to wear the bloomers, and when they did, they were made fun of. Susan wore it for

JOIN THE
NATIONAL

awhile, but people were paying too much attention to what she was wearing, and Susan was afraid they weren't paying serious attention to what she was saying. She decided to quit wearing the bloomers so people

would listen as she spoke about the importance for women to have the right to vote.

Susan traveled around the East giving speeches wherever people would listen. Sometimes people tore down the banners announcing her meetings. Sometimes men threw rotten eggs at her. Even certain women denounced her as "evil and shameless." But Susan would not give up.

She went from town to town in even the worst weather. She put up with poor food, sleepless nights, discomfort, sickness, and ridicule.

Finally, in 1865, the Thirteenth Amendment to the Constitution abolished slavery. One part of her battle was won. Then a new

Amendment to the constitution was put forth. It provided that all male citizens, regardless of color, had the right to vote, hold property, and exercise legal rights. Some other champions of women's rights were willing to accept this amendment. But not Susan. She demanded votes for women and Negroes alike.

Susan continued speaking, and she traveled around the country obtaining signatures for a petition which would be presented to the legislature. The petition called for the vote for women.

Nonetheless, the Fourteenth Amendment was proclaimed in 1868. Susan felt betrayed. The fight

for women's rights would have to begin all over again. She started a newspaper named REVOLUTION. For two years, it was the mouthpiece of the movement for women's suffrage—voting rights for women.

In 1869, Susan helped organize a Working Women's Association. With Elizabeth Cady Stanton, she also founded the National Woman Suffrage Association. The newspaper, REVOLUTION, and the Association were too outspoken for some women. Lucy Stone started a rival paper and a rival group. The women's rights movement suffered a split that would not be healed for many years.

Meanwhile, Susan had to give up her own newspaper, which was losing money. It almost broke her heart, but she fought on. She began traveling again, speaking and lecturing all over the country.

Susan decided to try a new approach in winning the right to vote. According to some lawyers, the Fourteenth Amendment already gave women the right to vote as citizens of the United States. In 1872, Susan decided to test this right. She cast a ballot on November 5, leading fifteen other women to do the same. On November 28, she was arrested by a United States marshal, and she was charged with voting illegally.

The trial of Susan B. Anthony was a nationwide sensation. The judge would not listen to her argu-

ments. He found Susan guilty and fined her $100. She told the judge, "I shall never pay a dollar of your unjust penalty." Quote

Susan never did pay her fine. The government dropped its case against the other fourteen women, also. The trial angered Susan, though, and she renewed her crusade with even greater vigor. All over the United States, women were listening to her, and finally, so were the men.

In the years that followed, state after state gave women the right to own property, to control their own money, and to share the guardianship of their children. But they still had not won the right to vote.

Susan and the other women decided they needed to reorganize

their efforts. In 1890, the two rival woman suffrage groups united into one. The first president of the new National American Woman Suffrage Association was Mrs. Stanton. The second was Susan B. Anthony. They worked tirelessly, and in the next ten years saw four states—Wyoming, Colorado, Idaho and Utah—give women the right to vote.

Susan was pleased about this, but she was also convinced that the only way for women in ALL states to win the right to vote was through a constitutional amendment. By this time, Susan was 80 years old. She continued working for the amendment until her death in 1906.

But Susan B. Anthony's dream did not die. Women continued to

work toward equality, and in 1920, just 100 years after Susan was born, Congress passed the Nineteenth Amendment which gave women in all states the right to vote. It is still known as the "Susan B. Anthony Amendment."

Women are still fighting to gain equal rights in the United States. Women have gained many rights and privileges since Susan B. Anthony worked for the Amendment granting women the right to vote. Times have changed, and women have changed, but no one can forget that Susan B. Anthony played a major role in changing attitudes about women and in gaining increased opportunities for women in American society.

WE THE PEOPLE SERIES

WOMEN OF AMERICA

CLARA BARTON
JANE ADDAMS
ELIZABETH BLACKWELL
HARRIET TUBMAN
SUSAN B. ANTHONY
DOLLEY MADISON

INDIANS OF AMERICA

GERONIMO
CRAZY HORSE
CHIEF JOSEPH
PONTIAC
SQUANTO
OSCEOLA

FRONTIERSMEN OF AMERICA

DANIEL BOONE
BUFFALO BILL
JIM BRIDGER
FRANCIS MARION
DAVY CROCKETT
KIT CARSON

WAR HEROES OF AMERICA

JOHN PAUL JONES
PAUL REVERE
ROBERT E. LEE
ULYSSES S. GRANT
SAM HOUSTON
LAFAYETTE

EXPLORERS OF AMERICA

COLUMBUS
LEIF ERICSON
DeSOTO
LEWIS AND CLARK
CHAMPLAIN
CORONADO